PHOTOGRAPHY EXPOSED

PAUL MEIGHAN and BERNARD McWILLIAMS

First published in Great Britain 1984
by **impact books**
112 Bolingbroke Grove, London SW11 1DA
Reprinted: 1984, 1985, 1987, 1988, 1989, 1990

ISBN 0–245–54106–3

Printed and bound in Great Britain by
The Guernsey Press Co. Ltd., Guernsey, Channel Islands.

CONTENTS

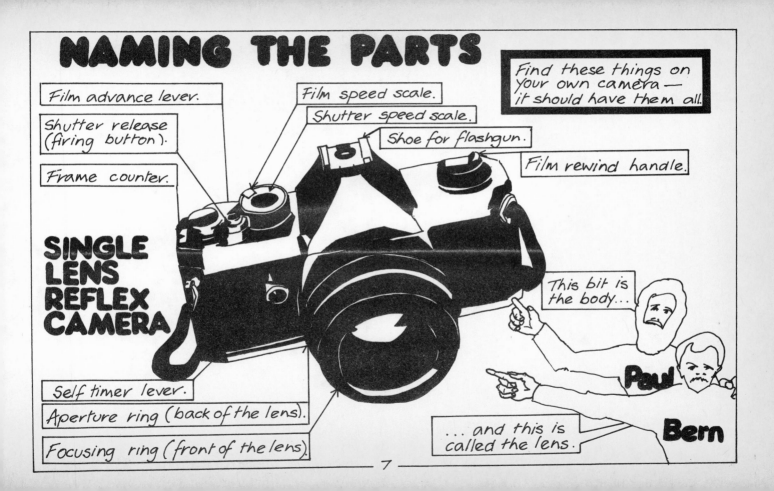

The first thing to do with your camera is PLAY WITH IT.

Twiddle all the knobs. Press all the buttons. Then open the back and play some more. Take off the lens and keep on playing.

Get used to turning the focusing ring and aperture ring while looking through your camera.

But NEVER go poking around inside — to a camera your fingers are horrible greasy things, so don't touch the glass of the lens, the shutter or the mirror.

This way you will become used to the feel of your camera.
You must be able to handle it CONFIDENTLY.

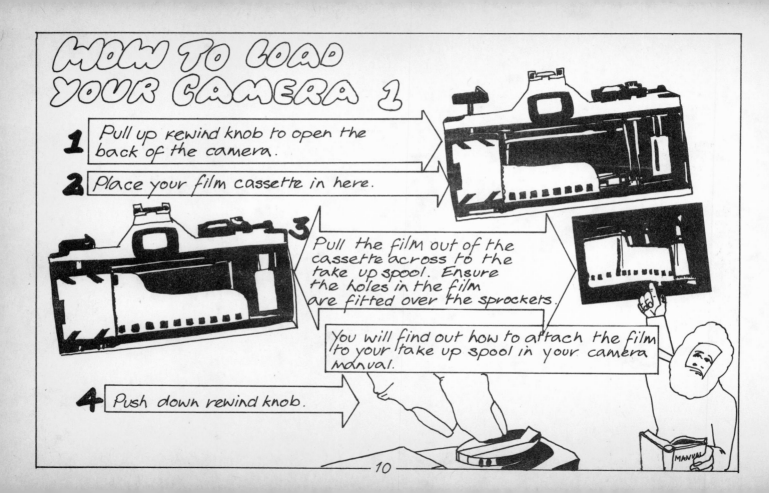

HOW TO LOAD YOUR CAMERA 3

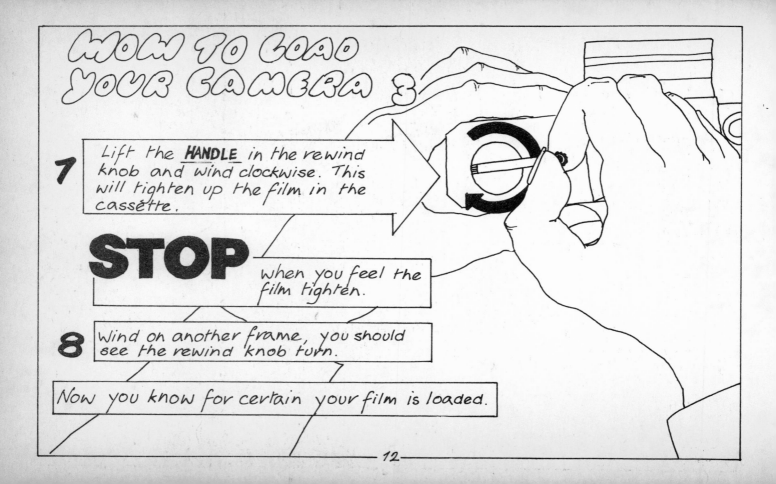

7 Lift the **HANDLE** in the rewind knob and wind clockwise. This will tighten up the film in the cassette.

STOP when you feel the film tighten.

8 Wind on another frame, you should see the rewind knob turn.

Now you know for certain your film is loaded.

Try to avoid loading your camera in strong light e.g. sunlight. If you have to load a film outside on a sunny day, turn your back to the sun and load your camera in the shade of your body.

HOW TO UNLOAD YOUR CAMERA

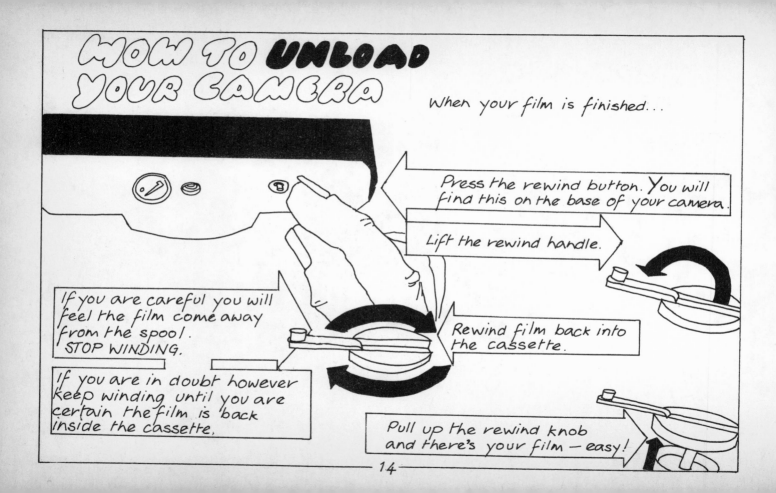

When your film is finished...

Press the rewind button. You will find this on the base of your camera.

Lift the rewind handle.

Rewind film back into the cassette.

If you are careful you will feel the film come away from the spool. STOP WINDING.

If you are in doubt however keep winding until you are certain the film is back inside the cassette.

Pull up the rewind knob and there's your film — easy!

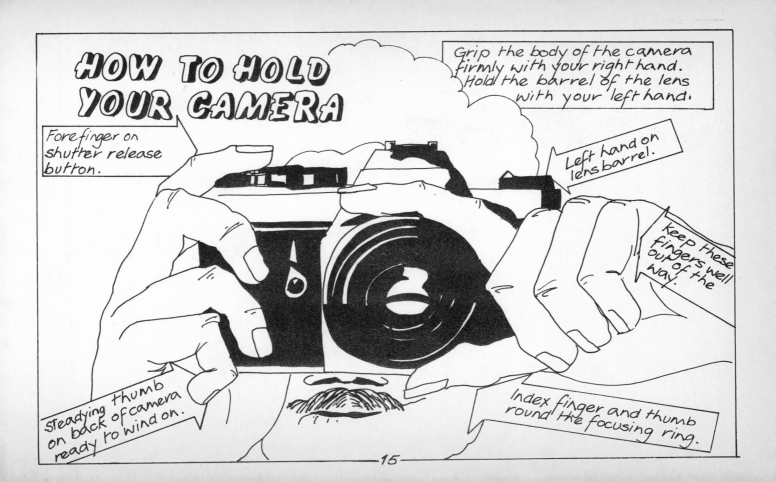

HOW TO HOLD YOUR CAMERA

You must avoid any movement of the camera during exposure.

ALWAYS press the shutter release GENTLY.

ALWAYS hold your breath when you fire the shutter.

ALWAYS tuck your elbows into your sides.

ALWAYS lean against a firm support if you can.

ALWAYS have both feet flat on the ground.

ALWAYS steady the camera as much as you can.

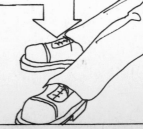

FOCUSING

This is easy, I just look in here and I can see through the lens.

Now I just turn the focusing ring until my subject comes into sharp focus.

Now this seems perfectly easy BUT always focus carefully.

ALWAYS go through the focus.
As the subject comes into focus keep turning the focusing ring until it starts to go out of focus again, THEN bring it back into focus.
KEEP doing this until you are sure your image is sharp.

Try and find a definite point or line on your subject to focus on.

It could be a lamp post or a reflection but try to find something.

If you are photographing a face you MUST focus on the eyes - or if you are close enough, on the one nearer the camera.

FOCUSING

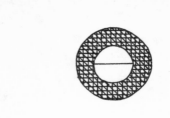

When you look into your camera you will probably see something like this.

The centre is the rangefinder spot.

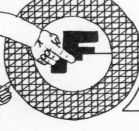

Turn the focusing ring until the two halves of the image meet.

The outside ring is the microprism and it allows faster focusing.

This should only be used when you need to focus quickly i.e. action photography.

THE SHUTTER

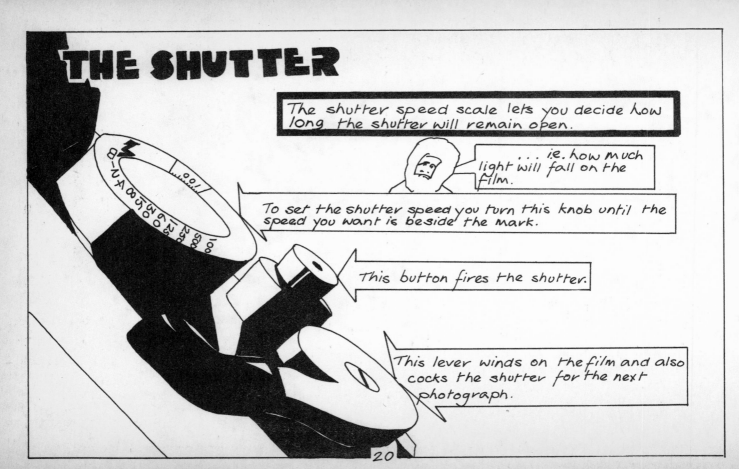

The shutter speed scale lets you decide how long the shutter will remain open.

...ie. how much light will fall on the film.

To set the shutter speed you turn this knob until the speed you want is beside the mark.

This button fires the shutter.

This lever winds on the film and also cocks the shutter for the next photograph.

SHUTTER SPEEDS

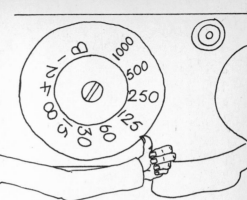

These numbers are all fractions of a second.

For example if you select this speed then your shutter will stay open for 1/125 of a second.

The B speed (at the top of the dial) means that the shutter will stay open as long as the shutter release button is depressed.

If you look carefully at these numbers you will notice that each is more or less half or double the number on either side.

This means that as you change to the next shutter speed you either double or halve the length of time the shutter will stay open.

1/500 halves that amount.

1/250 allows a certain amount of light onto the film.

1/125 doubles that amount.

THE SHUTTER

It is VERY easy for the camera to shake a little as you fire the shutter. This makes the photographs blurred.

SO use a fast shutter speed if you can

BUT if you must use a slow shutter speed:

Wrap the strap around your wrist...

...or set the camera on a flat surface...

...or press the camera against a wall....

...or rest your elbows on a firm surface...

...or use a tripod.

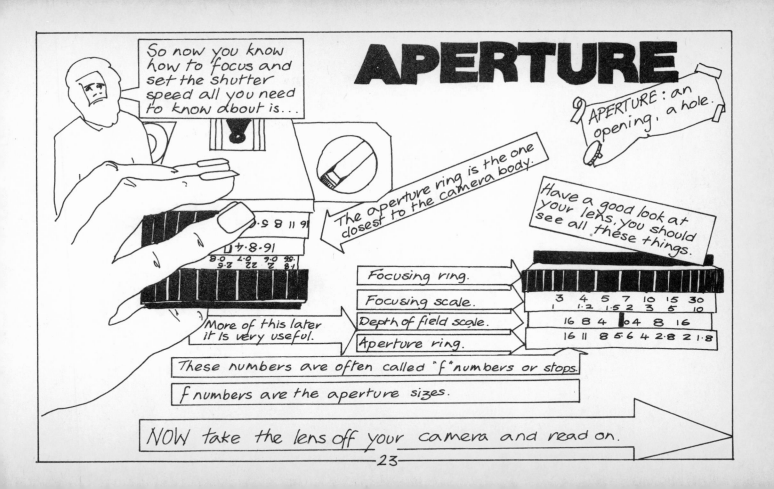

APERTURE

APERTURE

Set the aperture to the lowest number – usually f2 or f1·8.

Press the depth of field button on the side of your lens, or if you don't have one, press the pin that sticks out of the back of the lens.

Look through your lens.

f2

You will see that the hole for the light to pass through is as big as possible – FULL APERTURE.

Then set the aperture at the highest number – usually f16. There is now only a tiny hole for light to get through.

The f number tells you the size of the hole.

1·8   2   2·8   4   5·6   8   11   16

APERTURE

As you move to the next aperture you double or halve the amount of light that falls on your film.

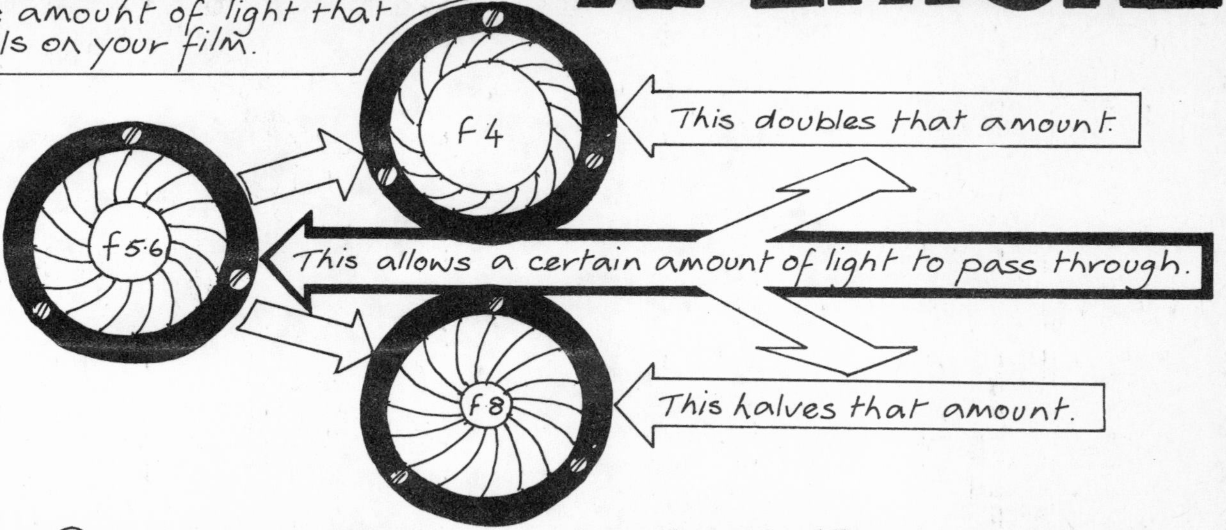

f 4

This doubles that amount.

f 5·6

This allows a certain amount of light to pass through.

f 8

This halves that amount.

So now we can control the amount of light that falls on the film in two ways — **SHUTTER SPEED** *and now* **APERTURE.**

EXPOSURE

SO how will you know what aperture and shutter speed to set?

Well your film must get just the right amount of light to form an image......

...or else your image will be too dark, UNDEREXPOSED...

...or too light, OVEREXPOSED.

You MUST use an aperture and shutter speed that will EXPOSE your film to the correct amount of light.

film speed

NOW ...

different films react to light at different speeds, so we say that films are either FAST or SLOW.

Before you use your camera metering or hand held meter you simply set the film speed on the FILM SPEED SCALE.

REMEMBER to do this,

especially when you load a new film of different speed.

WHEN

you have done this you can then measure the light.

There are two ways of measuring film speed— AMERICAN and EUROPEAN— both are usually given.

ISO 100 / 21°

This tells you the speed of the film— more of this later.

LIGHT METERS

The light from your subject must be measured by a *LIGHT METER*.

BUILT IN LIGHT METERS

Most S.L.R.s today have *LIGHT METERS* built into them. They measure the light that comes through the lens (T.T.L.).

You alter the aperture and shutter speed until the display in the viewfinder tells you that you have set them correctly.

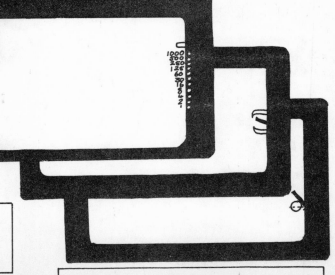

Common viewfinder displays.

LIGHT METERS

HAND HELD LIGHT METERS

Hand held meters are bought separately.

A hand held meter is pointed at the subject and a light value is indicated.

The complicated looking dials simply let you convert the light value (number) into a range of shutter speeds and apertures.

You simply select the most suitable combination and set them on your camera.

EASY!

HOW TO MEASURE LIGHT

The easiest way is just to point your camera at your subject.

Light is reflected from the subject.

You must always remember that the act of measuring light is totally separate from focusing or composing.

You must always measure the light FIRST !

HOW TO MEASURE LIGHT

BUT

you cannot expect your lightmeter to read your mind,

it can only read **LIGHT**.

THEREFORE...

think when you use your light meter.

CONSIDER THIS PICTURE

If you wanted to take a photograph like this you could not take an average light reading.

WHY NOT?

-31-

BECAUSE

most of the view is sky, which is very bright.

If you took an average reading your meter would give you a light reading to expose the sky correctly. But you want to photograph the PERSON.

He is the most important part of the picture and HE must be correctly exposed — if you took an average reading the figure would be UNDEREXPOSED.

Your meter cannot be expected to know this.

A great many photographs are wasted because of mistakes like this

HERE IS HOW TO AVOID THEM.

HOW TO MEASURE LIGHT

If there is a range of brightness in your picture, DECIDE what part is most important THEN...

1 Go close to your subject and measure the light from it...

Make sure you don't cast a shadow and measure that.

2 ...set your exposure controls...

APERTURE

SHUTTER SPEED

If your camera is on AUTOMATIC MODE this is when to use your EXPOSURE LOCK (if you have one).

3 ...compose and focus carefully, then fire the shutter.

The sky will be overexposed but the subject will be correctly exposed.

SO decide what is the most important part of your picture and expose for that.

MEASURE THE LIGHT ACCURATELY AND YOU CAN'T GO WRONG.

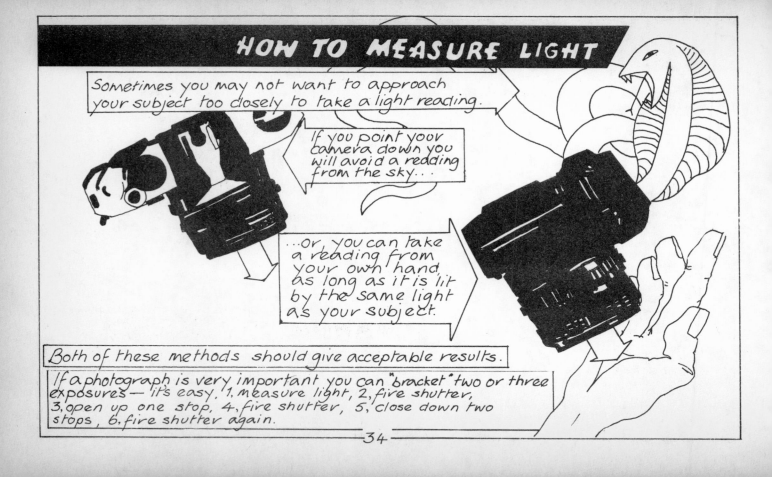

HOW TO MEASURE LIGHT

Sometimes you may not want to approach your subject too closely to take a light reading.

If you point your camera down you will avoid a reading from the sky...

...or, you can take a reading from your own hand, as long as it is lit by the same light as your subject.

Both of these methods should give acceptable results.

If a photograph is very important you can "bracket" two or three exposures — it's easy. 1. measure light, 2. fire shutter, 3. open up one stop, 4. fire shutter, 5. close down two stops, 6. fire shutter again.

AUTOMATIC EXPOSURE

Many cameras today have AUTOMATIC EXPOSURE controls. These are the main types.

APERTURE PRIORITY — with this system you simply set the aperture you want to use, then, when you measure the light (usually by pressing the shutter release button half way) the camera sets the shutter speed itself. There is usually an indication in the viewfinder of the shutter speed the camera has chosen.

SHUTTER PRIORITY — this system works the opposite way to APERTURE PRIORITY. This time you select the shutter speed you want and the camera selects the aperture. Again the camera's choice of aperture is usually displayed in the viewfinder.

This type of camera usually has an A on the APERTURE ring.

On this type of camera there is usually an A (AUTOMATIC) setting on the shutter speed dial.

MANUAL OVERRIDE

Most automatic cameras (but not all) allow you to set both exposure controls manually. When you do this you OVERRIDE the camera's automatic function.

For the serious amateur photographer MANUAL OVERRIDE is essential.

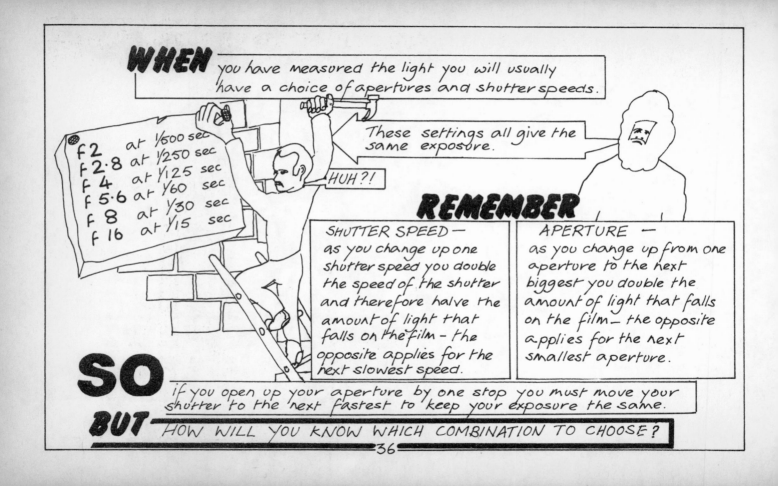

SHUTTER SPEEDS

Now you have to **THINK**

Slow speeds increase the risk of camera shake
Fast speeds reduce this risk.

BUT

There are times when you will want a slow speed - to show movement for example

and you will not always be able to use as fast a shutter speed as you would like.

For speeds of slower than 1/30 sec you should really use a tripod.

SHUTTER SPEEDS

Your lens will give its sharpest image if you keep away from very large or very small apertures.

BUT

to use an aperture in this range you might need to use a very slow shutter speed.

AND

this may not give you the DEPTH OF FIELD you want.

You must always consider the effect of the aperture you choose on DEPTH OF FIELD but more of this later.

f4 to f8 is the range your camera likes best.

If in doubt, opt for a fast shutter speed. Camera shake is more likely to cause loss of sharpness than a large aperture.

HOW TO TAKE A PHOTOGRAPH

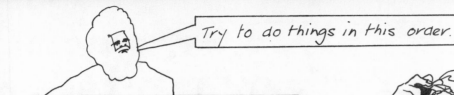

Try to do things in this order.

1-2-3-4.

1 MEASURE THE LIGHT.

2 SET EXPOSURE CONTROLS.

3 COMPOSE AND FOCUS.

4 FIRE SHUTTER.

BEWARE

With cameras which have built-in light meters it is tempting to combine stages 1-2-3. This will sometimes produce adequate results BUT NOT ALWAYS.

DEPTH OF FIELD

Remember how we focused on the most important part of the subject.

Well there is always an area in front of and behind the subject which is quite sharp, this is called.

DEPTH OF FIELD

See how the depth of field is divided so that 1/3 of it is in front of the subject and 2/3 behind it.

←— DEPTH OF FIELD —→

The camera is focused on the flower...

but the grass which is drawn in is also acceptably sharp and looks as if it too is in focus.

DEPTH OF FIELD

is **very important.** You can control it completely and you must know how.

DEPTH OF FIELD

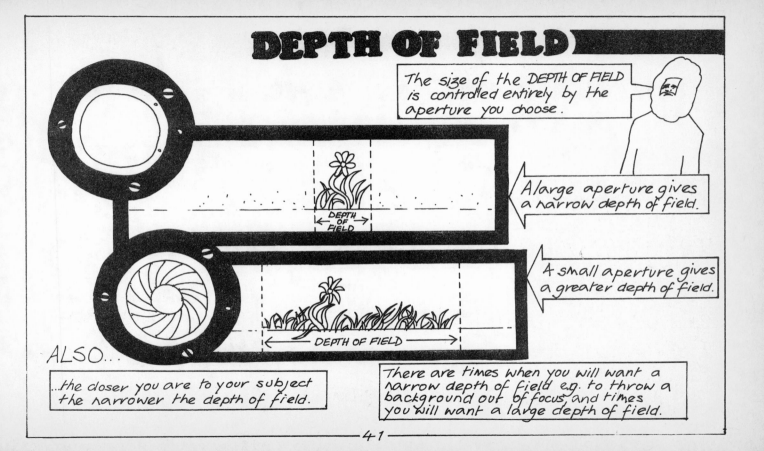

The size of the DEPTH OF FIELD is controlled entirely by the aperture you choose.

A large aperture gives a narrow depth of field.

A small aperture gives a greater depth of field.

ALSO...

...the closer you are to your subject the narrower the depth of field.

There are times when you will want a narrow depth of field e.g. to throw a background out of focus, and times you will want a large depth of field.

DEPTH OF FIELD

You can estimate your depth of field in two ways...

1. Once you have focused on your subject, press the DEPTH OF FIELD preview button on your lens. You will now see how much will be acceptably sharp.

2. Use the DEPTH OF FIELD SCALE on your lens — here's how.

The term acceptably sharp means different things to different people.

This Mark is the distance to your subject.

		This is depth of field.				
2	7	10 3	15 15		FT M
16	8 4	4	8	16	
16	11	8	5·6	4	2·8

This is the aperture you have set.

These are only approximate however.

Now if you look carefully you will see how this depth of field scale tells you that your subject is just over ten feet away and that at f8 your depth of field begins at seven feet and ends fifteen feet away from you.

film

1 You are interested only in 35mm film so you can ignore the rest.

At first sight the choice seems confusing but it's easy to sort out.

2 Decide if you want to use colour or black and white. If you choose to use black and white you can go straight to the next page.

3 choose If you choose to use colour

4 SLIDES

Buy REVERSAL film usually labelled "for slides"

These are also called transparencies

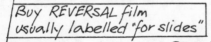

5 PRINTS

Buy NEGATIVE film. usually labelled "for prints"

One small point— always buy "DAYLIGHT" colour film even if you intend to use electronic flash. TUNGSTEN film is only for use with photoflood lights.

6 THEN decide how many exposures you want, usually 24 or 36.

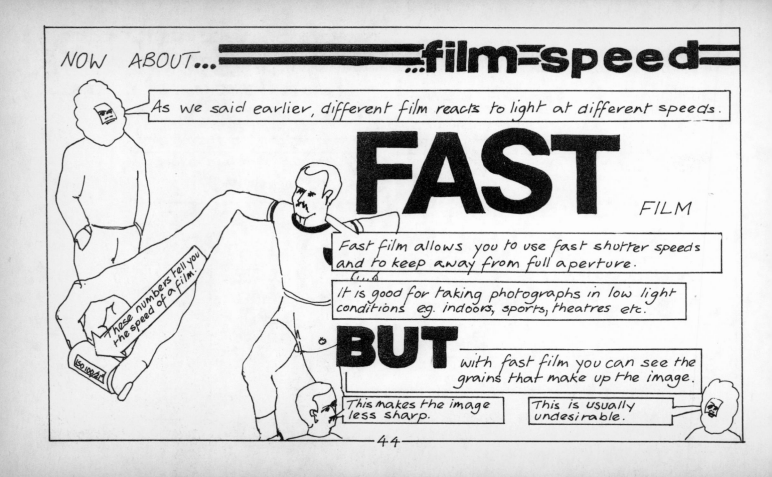

SLOW Film.

With slow film you will need a high level of light to avoid using slow shutter speeds.

BUT

slow film shows virtually no grain and therefore gives a very sharp image.

So what film should you use?

WHICH FILM

In **BLACK and WHITE** photography ILFORD offer three films
which are generally considered to be

SLOW	PAN F	50 A.S.A.
MEDIUM	FP4	125 A.S.A.
FAST	HP 5	400 A.S.A.

For **COLOUR SLIDE** film KODAK offer a large range of film.

SLOW	KODACHROME 25	25 A.S.A.
MEDIUM	KODACHROME 64	64 A.S.A
FAST	EKTACHROME 200	200 A.S.A.

For **COLOUR PRINT** film

MEDIUM	KODACOLOR VR 100	ISO 100.
FAST	KODACOLOR VR 400	ISO 400.

You will find at the end of this process that you have a choice of MANUFACTURERS and PRICES.
Try different ones. Find one you like and stay with it.
There are many other speeds and manufacturers of film. The ones on this page are
intended only as a guide.

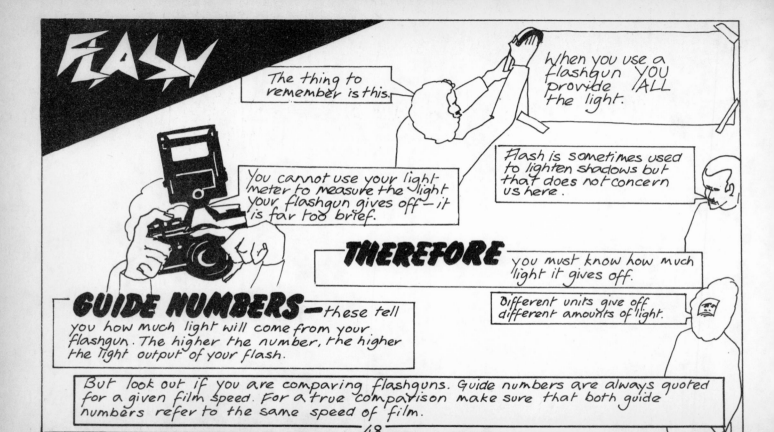

FLASH

The thing to remember is this.

When you use a flashgun YOU provide ALL the light.

Flash is sometimes used to lighten shadows but that does not concern us here.

You cannot use your light-meter to measure the light your flashgun gives off — it is far too brief.

THEREFORE

you must know how much light it gives off.

GUIDE NUMBERS —

these tell you how much light will come from your flashgun. The higher the number, the higher the light output of your flash.

Different units give off different amounts of light.

But look out if you are comparing flashguns. Guide numbers are always quoted for a given film speed. For a true comparison make sure that both guide numbers refer to the same speed of film.

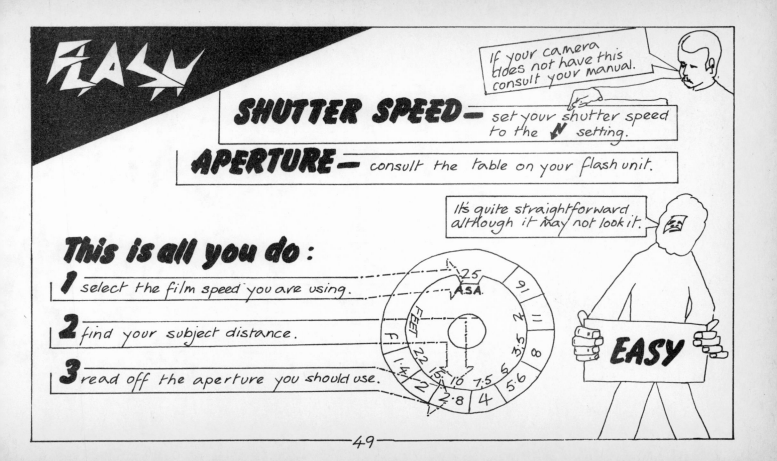

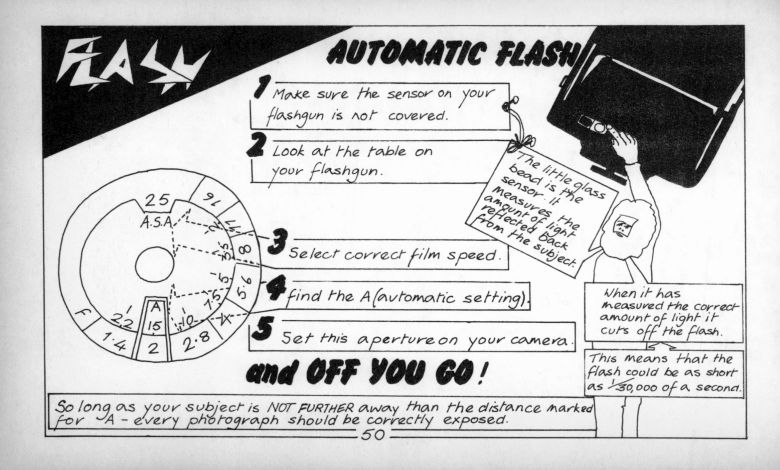

FLASH

AUTOMATIC FLASH

1 Make sure the sensor on your flashgun is not covered.

2 Look at the table on your flashgun.

3 Select correct film speed.

4 Find the A (automatic setting).

5 Set this aperture on your camera.

and OFF YOU GO!

The little glass bead is the sensor. It measures the amount of light reflected back from the subject.

When it has measured the correct amount of light it cuts off the flash.

This means that the flash could be as short as $\frac{1}{30,000}$ of a second.

So long as your subject is NOT FURTHER away than the distance marked for A – every photograph should be correctly exposed.

AUTOMATIC FLASH

THINK

You must always THINK when you use an automatic flash.

1 WATCH for dark backgrounds. Your automatic will try to light them and your subject will be overexposed.

2 BEWARE of changing lenses. Your automatic flash is designed primarily for standard lenses. With other lenses the automatic function may not be so reliable.

3 You can light subjects further away on manual mode. If you switch to manual and open your lens to full aperture you can light subjects further than the maximum distance on automatic. Your table will show you this.

REMEMBER. When you use your flash on manual you should cover the sensor.

FLASH

One way to avoid the harshness of flash light is to BOUNCE the flash light off a wall or ceiling - your automatic sensor should still function, so long as it remains pointed at the subject. You must be aware of the MAXIMUM distance your flash will cover (usually up to 40ft).

BOUNCED FLASH

← SENSOR DIRECTION

BE CAREFUL of coloured walls if you are using colour film.

BUT if this all sounds too good to be true it has **LOTS** of drawbacks.

Generally speaking flash kills all other light. If used on a camera it has all the subtlety of a searchlight being shone on the subject.

As a result it causes heavy black shadows behind your subject.

THE CURSE OF FLASH PHOTOGRAPHY:

Sometimes the pupils of eyes come out red in flash photographs.

RED EYES

This is caused by the flash being reflected by the blood vessels in the eye.

To avoid this you should hold the flash about a foot away from the camera.

LENSES

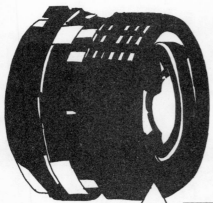

The lens which comes with your camera is called a **STANDARD** lens.

It is called a standard lens because it sees roughly the same amount of a scene as your eyes. The view of the subject does not change when you look through the lens. It looks neither closer nor further away.

The focal length is engraved on the front of the lens.

For 35mm photography the standard lens has a focal length of about 50mm.

Focal length is simply the distance from the centre of the lens to the film when the lens is focused on INFINITY.

LENSES

What are AUTOMATIC LENSES?

These lenses allow you to set the aperture.

BUT when you do so the aperture does NOT get smaller.

When you fire the shutter the aperture is stopped down the instant the shutter is opened SO you always focus at full aperture ie. with a bright image.

What about LENS MOUNTS?

screw — using this method, lenses are simply screwed into the camera body. Thread sizes vary. Changing lenses is quite a slow business.

Sadly there is no standard fitting.

bayonet — using this method the lens is placed into grooves in the camera body. A quarter turn locks the lens. Lens changing is very fast.

So before buying a new lens make sure it fits!

What do different lenses do?

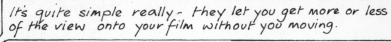

It's quite simple really — they let you get more or less of the view onto your film without you moving.

So **telephoto** *lenses take you closer to your subject.*

Wide angle *lenses make your subject look further away.*

warning warning

Before you buy a lens or any other piece of equipment: BE SURE YOU HAVE A USE FOR IT. Do NOT buy a lens in the hope that it will take better pictures or make you look professional

Here is a GOLDEN RULE. Only part with your money when you NEED a piece of equipment. Follow this rule and you will use all your equipment and will not fall for flashy advertisements or sales talk.

TELEPHOTO—

a lens with a focal length greater than that of a standard lens (it is also called a long focus or long lens).

As we have already said a TELEPHOTO lens takes a small part of your view and makes it fill your frame.

Why not just move closer?

1 sometimes you will not be able to go closer ie. when photographing BIRDS, ANIMALS, CANDIDS etc.

2 AND if you move closer you change the perspective of your photograph and there are times when this is undesirable.

It's o.k., perspective is explained.

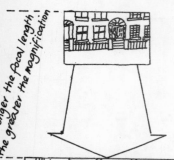

The longer the focal length the greater the magnification

TELEPHOTO LENS

The DEPTH OF FIELD gets narrower as you increase the focal length. So focusing must be more precise than usual.

If you want to photograph a subject close up (head and shoulders) you must use a telephoto lens to avoid distortion.

LENSES

TELEPHOTO—135 mm.

WHAT SIZE IS BEST?

You should be able to answer this yourself.

Extreme telephoto lenses are very dramatic and very expensive. But when would you use one?

ALSO- the longer the focal length the heavier the lens and so the more difficult to hold steady.

AND- as the focal length gets longer your widest aperture gets smaller.

So what's so magical about this focal length

It offers a reasonable maximum aperture.

Nothing of course it's just a compromise.

But it's a pretty good compromise.

It is still long enough to avoid close up distortion in head and shoulders portraits.

Depth of field is good.

It does offer a "close up" view of your subject.

Convention now dictates that the 135mm is the standard TELEPHOTO.

It does not have to be an expensive item to buy.

Before we say any more about lenses, let us look at **PERSPECTIVE**.

a STANDARD LENS.

The subject is closer to the camera than the passing elephant so he appears to be taller than the elephant.

The relative size of these objects is distorted but we are used to these distortions and see them as normal.

Look what happens when you take a photograph of the same subject and background from a long way off.

STANDARD LENS FROM FAR AWAY.

Here the camera is far away from the subject and so both appear their proper size.

TELEPHOTO LENS FROM FAR AWAY.

If you use a TELEPHOTO lens there seems to be very little distance between the subject and the background.

N.B. the lens has not altered the perspective — only changing the camera position can change the perspective.

This is why people sometimes say that TELEPHOTO lenses flatten perspective.

wide angle

A lens with a focal length shorter than that of a standard lens is called a WIDE ANGLE LENS.

The shorter the focal length the wider the angle of view.

STANDARD LENS

WIDE ANGLE LENS

As we have said, a wide angle lens takes in more of the view.

Why not just move away from the subject to get more of it into view?

BECAUSE ...

wide angle

Sometimes you may not be able to get far enough away from your subject i.e. indoors.

Wide angle lenses are not used for portraits unless you want to use the distortion they cause.

With wide angle lenses the depth of field is much greater than that offered by standard lenses so focusing does not have to be so precise.

It is easy to see why many news photographers like wide angle lenses. They get a wide angle view of the subject AND they can focus quickly.

wide angle   LENSES

35mm and 28mm are the most popular wide angle lenses.

BUT

there are some things you must watch if you use a wide angle lens.

1 Beware of distortion caused by going too close to the subject.

2 If you tilt your camera upwards vertical lines will converge.

AND THERE'S MORE

wide angle

3 If you use a flash gun with a wide angle lens the flash may not cover your whole field of view.

Area covered by lens.

Area covered by flash.

FISH-EYE LENSES.

These are extreme wide angle lenses. Some have an angle of view of 180°.

They form a massively distorted image on film.

Their depth of field is so great that they do not need to be focused!

perspective

LENSES

STANDARD LENS

Let's start from this picture again

The subject appears large because he is close to the camera.

NOW

If you put a WIDE ANGLE lens on your camera you get more of the scene into the picture.

WIDE ANGLE LENS

With the wide angle lens still on your camera go close to your subject until he fills the frame.

The wide angle lens exaggerates the distortion of the first picture because the subject is now closer to the camera.

WIDE ANGLE LENS FROM CLOSE UP.

There appears to be a considerable distance between subject and background.

If you go really close with a wide angle lens you get this kind of distortion. Those parts of the face nearest the camera appear much larger than the rest of the face.

REMEMBER THIS!

It is sometimes said therefore that a wide angle lens exaggerates perspective — again you know what it really does.

63

MACRO LENSES

Some lenses have a macro facility. They allow you to focus very close to your subject.

The closer you can get to your subject, the larger it's image will be on your film.

So these lenses are very useful for close up photography.

While you can get this facility on lenses with a range of focal lengths, such lenses have a smaller maximum aperture than comparable conventional lenses.

Cameras are expensive items.

To repair them is also expensive.

So always take care of your camera

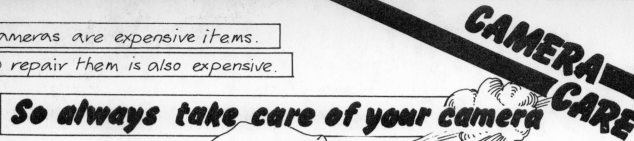

CAMERA CARE

BLOWER BRUSH

This is what you want to keep your camera in tip top condition.

PHOTOGRAPHIC LENS TISSUE

With a blower brush you can brush up any dust, grit or pieces of broken film and blow them out of your camera.

NEVER touch the bristles of the brush with your fingers. If you do, you will put grease on the bristles and then onto your camera.

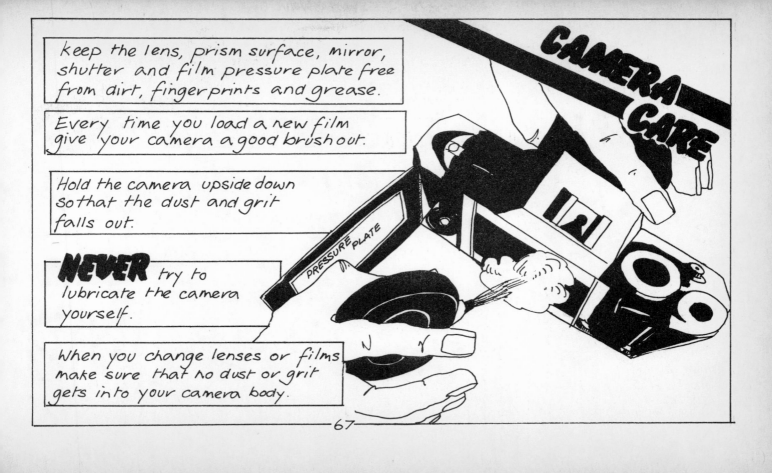

keep the lens, prism surface, mirror, shutter and film pressure plate free from dirt, fingerprints and grease.

Every time you load a new film give your camera a good brush out.

Hold the camera upside down so that the dust and grit falls out.

NEVER try to lubricate the camera yourself.

When you change lenses or films make sure that no dust or grit gets into your camera body.

NEVER use your finger or handkerchief to clean your lens.

ALWAYS use lens tissues.

BUT you can clean your lens too often. You may rub off the coating on your lens.

The lens coating is put there to reduce the light reflection from the lens — to give a sharper picture.

NEVER use force on any of the controls of your camera. If you need force you are doing something wrong.

keep your camera away from very hot places (like the glove compartment of a car on a hot day).

CAMERA CARE

Too much heat affects the lubrication in the camera and can even loosen bits inside the camera.

If you do not intend to use your camera for a while ...

DON'T leave the shutter cocked,

DON'T leave film in the camera,

DON'T leave batteries in the camera.

ON THE BEACH

You must keep sand away from your camera at all costs.

keep your camera wrapped up inside a polythene bag until you want to use it.

Protect your camera from salt spray.

IF you should ever drop your camera into the sea,

FIRST rinse it thoroughly in fresh water,

then take it for repair **QUICKLY!**

EXTRAS EXTRAS
GETTING CLOSE

CLOSE UP LENSES — these are screwed onto the front of the lens they are basically just magnifying lenses.

REVERSING RING — this allows you to mount your lens back to front on your camera body.

It lets you focus closer to your subject.

EXTRAS EXTRAS
BELLOWS & EXTENSION TUBES

These are used for close up photography. The closer a lens is to a subject, the larger the image will be on a film.

Few lenses can focus if they are closer than about nine inches from a subject (except MACRO lenses of course).

Bellows are mounted between the body and the lens. These offer you total control over exactly how close you want your lens to be.

If you use bellows with a MACRO lens, you can get extremely close.

Extension tubes normally come in sets of three.

Extension tubes can be screwed together in any combination and fit between body and lens.

SO BELLOWS and EXTENSION TUBES allow you to move your lens closer to the subject.

EXTRAS EXTRAS

AUTO WINDERS

Many cameras can now be fitted with AUTO WINDERS. which automatically wind on the film and cock the shutter after each exposure.

They make it possible to expose about two frames per second.

So they are very useful for action photography.

BE CAREFUL, it is very easy to waste a lot of film with an autowinder.

Remember

One of the most important decisions photographers make is exactly when to fire the shutter. YOU are much more competent to judge this than a machine.

MOTOR DRIVES

MOTOR DRIVES are professionals' tools. They can shoot up to nine frames per second and are very expensive.

EXTRASEXTRAS
filters

These are pieces of glass which are screwed onto the front of the lens.

Here are the main types and what they do.

ultraviolet

Ultraviolet filters reduce the amount of ultraviolet light that falls on your film, reducing the amount of haze in scenic views.

Ultraviolet filters need no extra exposure. Many photographers leave this filter permanently on to protect the lens.

polarizing

Polarizing filters work like polaroid sunglasses. They reduce the amount of reflection from water and other shiny surfaces (but not metal). They also darken blue skies—especially if pointed at right angles to the sun.

You can turn these filters in front of the camera to control the amount of reflection you want to remove.

skylight

Skylight filters do much the same as ultraviolet but are designed specifically for colour.

EXTRAS EXTRAS
filters

Be careful

Be sure to buy the right size of filter for the lens you intend to use it on!

neutral density

Neutral density filters simply reduce the amount of light reaching the film, enabling you to use a wider aperture or slower shutter speed.

filter factors

These numbers are quoted for all filters. They tell you how much extra light you must allow into your camera when using them e.g. a filter with a factor of 2x needs double the amount of light so you must open up by one stop or move up one shutter speed.

IF you use a through the lens metering camera, it will automatically compensate for any filter you use.

EXTRAS EXTRAS
filters

In **black & white** photography

Colour is reduced to tones of grey.

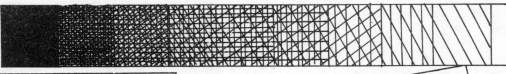

Here is the effect produced by some coloured filters on black and white film.

No. 15 DEEP YELLOW   darkens blue and makes clouds stand out in a blue sky.

NO. 25 RED   reduces landscape haze.

No. 58 GREEN   lightens green to show detail in foliage.

These are just a few — there are many more for you to try.

EXTRASEXTRAS

TRIPODS

Tripods are used to steady your camera when you use a slow shutter speed.

Once the camera is mounted on the tripod you can leave the shutter open for as long as you like – THERE WILL BE NO CAMERA SHAKE!

BUT do not press the shutter release button with your finger, this will move the camera. ———— USE A CABLE RELEASE.

This screw goes into the hole in the camera base.

If you want to buy a tripod – it MUST be sturdy – its function is to hold the camera steady.

Screw one end of the cable release into the hole in the shutter release button then PRESS to fire.

COMPOSITION

You must LOOK and THINK.

The most expensive camera in the world won't help with this.

You must know exactly why you are taking a photograph.

COMPOSITION

First **THINK** — what exactly do you want to communicate with your picture?

Then **LOOK** through the camera - arrange the elements of your picture to communicate the purpose of your picture.

These do not need to be very grand. You may wish to communicate the happiness of a party or the desolation of a moor.

The choice is infinite and it is all yours. This freedom is the joy of the amateur photographer.

COMPOSITION

Here are a few guidelines but remember there are no hard and fast rules.

1 ALWAYS have a centre of interest in your picture.

Try to avoid putting the centre of interest in the middle of your picture. **2**

This is a better picture.

3 ALWAYS avoid the horizon cutting your picture in half.

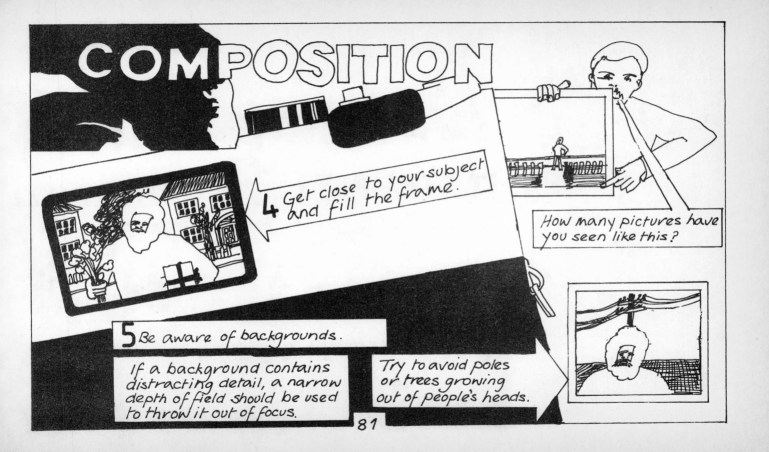

COMPOSITION

4 Get close to your subject and fill the frame.

How many pictures have you seen like this?

5 Be aware of backgrounds.

If a background contains distracting detail, a narrow depth of field should be used to throw it out of focus.

Try to avoid poles or trees growing out of people's heads.

81

COMPOSITION

6 KEEP IT STRAIGHT!

A.

B.

B is a picture,
A is a joke!

Use lines to lead your
eye into your picture.

The line of the fence leads your
eye into the picture.

C.

D.

7

AVOID straight lines coming from the bottom
of your picture. C is fine, D is not so good.

COMPOSITION

8 **FRAME** your subject if you can.

Framing is often useful in filling "empty" skies.

9 Don't take all your photographs from the obvious angle. Bend your knees sometimes.

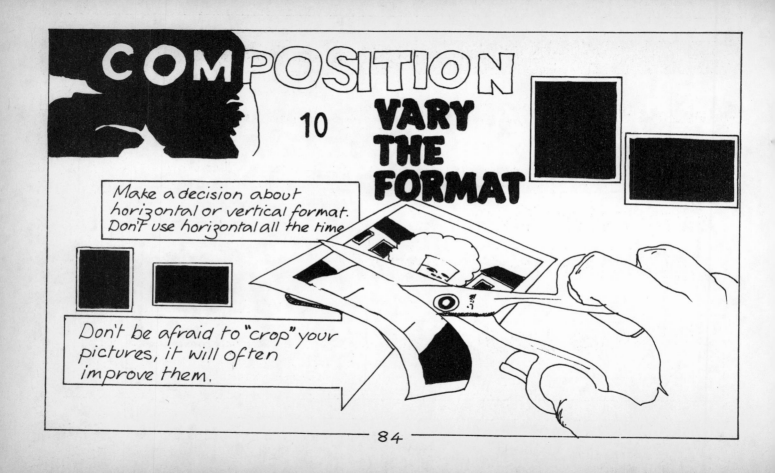

COMPOSITION

10 VARY THE FORMAT

Make a decision about horizontal or vertical format. Don't use horizontal all the time

Don't be afraid to "crop" your pictures, it will often improve them.

JARGON

A SURVIVAL GUIDE

ASA — American Standards Association — Numerical indication of film speed. They are defunct now but we still use their initials.

AUTOMATIC CAMERA — A camera which automatically selects the aperture and/or shutter speed.

CENTRE WEIGHTED METER — A meter which is more sensitive to the central area of the viewfinder.

CHANGING BAG — A light tight bag used to handle photographic material in total darkness. It is very handy if you have to open your camera with a film still inside.

JARGON

COATED LENS

A lens with a coating on the surface to improve picture quality by reducing flare.

That's what makes the lens look blue.

DEDICATED FLASH

This is usually of the same manufacture as the camera. Information about the flash is displayed in the camera viewfinder — it can tell you if the flash is switched on and if it has fired.

DIAPHRAGM

The aperture mechanism which determines the size of the aperture.

It acts just like the iris of an eye.

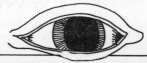

JARGON

DIN — Deutsche Industrie Norm – the European standard for film speeds.

ELECTRONIC SHUTTER — A shutter which is powered by a battery rather than the usual spring.

FLARE — Flare is the result of light shining directly on the surface of the lens and can cause reduced contrast and bright misty patches on a photograph.

A lens hood will help to avoid this.

FOCAL PLANE SHUTTER — This is a shutter built into the body of the camera, just in front of the film plane.

As opposed to a between the lens shutter which is built into the lens.

JARGON

FOCAL PLANE FLASH METERING

This does of course require a dedicated flash.

This is a method of measuring the reflected light from the subject at the focal plane. This means that provided the flash can cover a wide area, automatic flash control should work with a wide range of lenses.

ISO

International Standards Organisation - a numbering system in which the speed of a film is in both ASA and Din e.g. ISO 100/21°.

LED

Light emitting diode — found also in amplifiers etc.
Sometimes LEDs are used for readouts in camera viewfinders.

JARGON

LENS ELEMENTS

These are the individual pieces of glass which make up a lens. The number of elements in a modern lens can be as few as two or as many as twenty!

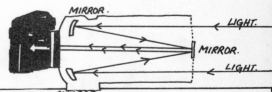

MIRROR.

LIGHT.

MIRROR.

LIGHT.

MIRROR.

MIRROR LENS

These are telephoto lenses which are short and fat rather than long and thin. They have a fixed aperture. Their proper name is CATADIOPTIC lenses.

OPEN APERTURE METERING

So that the image stays bright.

This means that as you alter the f number when taking an exposure reading the lens remains at full aperture. It is also called FULL APERTURE METERING.

PANCHROMATIC

This word describes BLACK and WHITE film which is sensitive to all colours of light.

PRINT

A piece of photographic paper with a positive image.

PROGRAMMED MODE

You just aim focus and fire

An exposure control which automatically selects factory programmed combinations of aperture and shutter speed according to the camera's exposure reading.

JARGON

RING FLASH — An electronic flash unit mounted on the front of the lens. It produces no shadows and is mainly used for close up work.

STOP-DOWN METERING — This means that as you alter the "f" number when taking an exposure reading, the lens stops down to the "f" number selected.

It means that the image gets dim.

ZOOM FLASH — An electric flash unit with a reflector head that can be adjusted to spread the flash to suit wide angle, standard and telephoto lenses.

INDEX—

Strap 9.22.

Telephoto lenses 55.56.57.58

Tripod 22.37.77.

T.T.L. 28.

Tungsten film 43.

Under exposure 26.

Unloading a camera 14.

Viewfinder displays 28.

Wide angle lenses 55.59-62.

Zoom flash 91.

Zoom lens 65.